Odds and Ends

Un   *t* ®

Un   *t* ®

ODDS AND ENDS.

COSTANÇA,

A POEM

Un   *t* ®

𝔍𝔫 𝔙𝔢𝔯𝔰𝔢 𝔞𝔫𝔡 𝔓𝔯𝔬𝔰𝔢.

BY

WILLIAM HENRY MERLE, ESQ.

ILLUSTRATED BY GEORGE CRUIKSHANK,

FROM DESIGNS BY THE AUTHOR.

LONDON·

PRINTED FOR
LONGMAN, REES, ORME, BROWN, AND GREEN,
PATERNOSTER ROW.

1831.

LONDON
S Manning & Co Printers, London house Yard, St Paul's

CONTENTS.

––––

* I am induced to add a note myself, finding how few persons are aware that the Bullfinch in a state of nature does not sing—it has but one soft melancholy note, at least, such is the idea it conveys to the human ear The poor birds which are kept in prison by our "gentle fair," owe their musical talent to the arts of education, or that more brutal act of cruelty, piercing the brilliant black eye of Bully with a red-hot needle

ILLUSTRATIONS.

* The designs which accompany the "Arab Gray," are entirely due to the invention of Cruikshank. Having taken a fancy to the subject, they were given up to the devices of his pencil.

Un   *t* ®

THE LOVES

OF

A PIG AND A CAT.

Un   *t* ®

THE LOVES OF A PIG AND A CAT.

𝔄 𝔗𝔞𝔩𝔢.

FOUNDED IN FACT.

DESCEND, ye Nine! on tuneful wing:
  Ye Nine!—not less than that—
For love's my theme: the love I sing
  Between a Pig and Cat.

Forbear your smile!—where'er it grow,
  Love's still a thing divine.
A jewel's still a jewel, though
  It grace the snout of swine.

There lived a Pig,—the date we pass
  For reasons strong and clear,
Let one suffice—that I, alas!
  Have never heard the year.

Of Piggy's death one fatal day
   The fame has long survived;
And therefore I make bold to say,
   Before his death—he lived.—

He lived, I'm sure,—and sure 't is true
   There also lived a Kitten;
And short the time, before the two
   Were mutually smitten.

Whence sprang this love the learned doubt,
   Conjectures scarce avail;
Puss perhaps was smitten with his snout,—
   Perhaps tickled by his tail.—

But what could pierce the living flitch,
   And Piggy's heart attach?
Unless that Pigs are prone to itch,
   And Kittens apt to scratch.

Howe'er it was,—round Pig and Cat
   Affection linked her chain;
But how they learned to love and chat,
   May never be so plain.

Uni   ℍ ®

They deeply loved—if it be love,
   In every hour and weather,
To eat, to drink, to lie, to rove,
   And always sleep together.

And thus awhile their moments flew
   In bliss no wealth could buy;
And Pussy purred, while Piggy drew
   His grunt of luxury.

But cruel man of love makes light,
   Compassion meets a dead stop,
When hunger prompts an appetite
   For bacon, or a pork-chop.

The Farmer deemed such love a whim,
   Gross profit filled his head;
The only thought that weighed with him,
   Was Piggy's weight when dead.

And woe to Alderman or Hog,
   Whom feasting renders fatter;
Death fells the former, like a log,
   The butcher sticks the latter.

Uni   ft ®

And vain alike were prayers and squeaks
  Of two as pure as lambs—
Poor Piggy's head was turned to cheeks,
  His legs walked into hams!

Yet why the mournful tale pursue,
  How Pig was hung and quartered,
Enough—too much—to know it true
  That he indeed was slaughtered.

He died: and death to Piggy gave
  That rest he gives to man,
For feeling dwells not in the grave,—
  Nor in the pickle-pan.

Uni   *ft ®*

But how describe that fatal day,
   Poor Pussy's frantic cry ;
When all she loved was torn away,
   And Pig was doomed to die?

Puss had no words; but, ah ! her look,
   Her mien, her anguish spake ;
Despair was there—'t was Nature's book,
   Which told the heart would break.

What now to Puss was pity's voice,
   The parlour rug for bed,
The varied meats to tempt her choice ?
   Could these restore the dead !—

She scorned them all;—He was not nigh
   To share the proffered cheer,
And what is life without the tie
   Which made existence dear.

Ah ! what indeed, but one cold blank
   From which the wretched shrink !
A desert spot, where all is rank—
   Puss would not eat nor drink.

c

Lives must be fed, though nine they be,—
   And Cats have nine, we know;—
The worm can pierce the hardest tree,
   The strongest bend to woe.

And withering hope had sown its blight
   Within poor Pussy's breast,
As still she watched by day and night
   The haunts by memory blest.

And there she sat, till faintly rose
   Life's last, and fluttering tide;
Then all was hushed in calm repose,
   The heart was broke—she died!

———

If Piggy's tale has tickled me,
   And roused a sportive vein;
'Tis as from thought the wretched flee
   By making light of pain.

Uni   ft ®

My heartless mirth intends no sneer;
   I vow by earth and heaven,
Had I the power to shed a tear,
   To Puss it should be given!

This cannot be; yet from her fate—
   Although the moral's dry—
I'll preach, and say—"Go, IMITATE
   A CAT'S FIDELITY!"

Note.—The habits and peculiarities of animals are always interesting when we know them to be well authenticated, and I cannot refrain from relating the following instance of singular attachment. In the latter part of March, 1830, an ewe in the flock of Robert Pattison, Esq., Dorset, died in yeaning

a male lamb of unusual size. The lamb survived, and was
taken up by the shepherd, and carried by him to the dairy-
house, to be brought up by hand. As, however, the lamb
appeared to be particularly strong and healthy, the shepherd
thought he would try if he could induce him to draw milk
from a cow which had calved that day. The trial succeeded,
and in a short time he was brought to suck without assistance.
For three days the lamb and the calf were suckled together
without distinction. The calf was then taken away, and the
cow immediately fixed her affection solely on the little change-
ling, as she did not shew any of the usual signs of uneasiness
at the loss of her own offspring. From that time the cow and
lamb were inseparable companions. The lamb would distin-
guish her from all the other cows which fed in the same
pasture, would bleat after her as his own dam, and was always
answered by the lowing of his step-mother, who, when driven
with the rest of her companions to be milked night and morning, could never be persuaded to leave the yard without him.
She generally suckled him in a standing posture: and this was
not attended with difficulty to either, as the lamb stood high
on his legs when first born, and grew rapidly in consequence
of the great increase of nourishment. How long this extraordinary attachment would have continued is uncertain, as the
experiment was not carried beyond the third month At that
period it became necessary to change the pasture of the cows,

and they were driven to the water-meadows—a land of plenty for the cows, who eat and thrive; but fatal to sheep, who eat and die, becoming in a short time coathed, and victims to a disease for which no remedy has hitherto been discovered Sad, alas! was the alternative for the pet lamb: nothing remained but the Irish humanity of Pat, who killed his horse to save it from dying: as in poor Piggy's case, the butcher's knife became the instrument of death. The shepherd adds, that the cow was not reconciled to the loss of her little nurseling for many days after the separation. she bellowed incessantly, and ran to and fro in search of him, with every demonstration of restlessness and anxiety in her look and manner; and a considerable time elapsed before she settled down into her wonted quiet. To the farmer it may be interesting to know, that the lamb weighed fourteen pounds the quarter to the epicure, that the meat was exquisitely fine.

The friend who favoured me with the above particulars, added another anecdote, equally well authenticated, and which, though somewhat foreign to the purpose, I shall add, as illustrating the habits of birds, and because it will lead me to relate an extraordinary combat which I witnessed between four ravens.

LOVE AND WAR.

"A battle between two crows was witnessed by some men work-
ing in a saw-pit, near Dorchester. Two crows (a male and a
female, it is presumed) were seen to alight in a water-meadow,
separated only by a small rivulet from the field in which the
men were at work · shortly afterwards, a third crow joined
the former two. The intrusion was ill-timed—it was presently
resented—love gave place to war, and a desperate conflict
ensued between the rival compeers, who buffeted each other
with their wings, and used their beaks and claws with all the
courage and determination of two game cocks The fight was
renewed at intervals, and lasted, upon the whole, nearly half an
hour. Meanwhile the female continued hovering over-head,
wheeling round and round, and occasionally darting down
upon the combatants; whether for the purpose of animating or
suspending the fray could not be determined. At length one
of the sawyers, perceiving that the hostilities had ceased,
walked up to the scene of action. One bird he found lying on
his breast quite dead, his feathers dirty and much stained with
blood, which flowed from a wound in his thigh, the bone of
which was completely crushed.* The other had suffered so
severely, and was so far exhausted, that being unable to effect

---

* My friend, with his usual ingenuity, has preserved the rival warriors

his escape, he was taken and executed on the spot, without
regard to the courtesy of arms. The female crow flew off at
the approach of the man, but soon returned again, and was
observed during the remaining part of the day, sitting on the
neighbouring trees, lamenting with hoarse and dissonant cries
the untimely fate of her lost companions."

THE FOUR RAVENS.

SOME years since, while living in Surry, my attention was
attracted by an unusual " croaking of the raven," or rather by
that peculiar sound which is familiar to the ear of every
sportsman, and is instantly recognised as the cry of war. Upon
quitting the house, I perceived four ravens upon wing, between
whom hostilities had commenced: they continued to skirmish
for some time, each struggling to gain the upper hand, and
strike upon the enemy beneath; before long, however, they
came to close quarters, and soon were so interwoven and
matted together that they were either unable, or, in the bitter-
ness of anger, forgot to make use of their wings, without which
aid not Icarus, nor the flying American, could evade the laws
of gravitation—neither could the ravens: down they came, and
tumbled   ther, he

Uni   ft ®

rallied his forces, and in a few minutes the four combatants were made prisoners, and this too without receiving a wound, an escape which rarely happens when opposed to the power of a raven's beak in fact, the four birds were so completely absorbed in the spirit of contest, that, as "the Billy's" master would have said, "it was a hard matter to choke them off" I presented two of the captives to a neighbour; and gave to the remaining two the range of our garden, where they remained a long time, and would have done so much longer, had not a gardener endeavoured to make certainty doubly sure, and seeing how effectually flight was prevented by clipping one wing, in the infinity of his wisdom clipped two wings equally. The consequences may be foreseen. as the feathers grew, both wings became equally strong, and the prisoners escaped over their walls. As they were never seen nor heard of afterwards, it is fair to presume that during their confinement they gained wisdom, and having had ample leisure to reflect "what a couple of old fools we were," they contrived to live in peace and harmony for the rest of their days.—No bad hint to man himself.

TO THE

WILD BULLFINCH,

AND THOSE WHO KNOW HIM IN THE WOODS.

Uni   *ft* ®

Uni   *ft* ®

TO

THE WILD BULLFINCH,

AND THOSE WHO KNOW HIS NOTE IN THE WOODS.

———

BULLY, sweet bird, I love thy note
   Of wildest minstrelsy,
When thou dost tune thy murmuring throat,
   And art at liberty.—

Thou art the fairies' mournful lyre
   Which tells of broken vows,
When they from frolic mirth retire
   To weep amidst the boughs;

Thou art the zephyr's softest breath
   Which sighs along the gale,
When zephyrs raise for summer's death
   Their melancholy wail;

Uni   ft ®

It is the spirit of the leaves
   Which lingers near the dead,
And though thy beak of sable grieves
   For life and beauty fled.

For this, and for thy melody,
   Thy soft and plaintive tone,
I 'll love thee, Bully, till I die,—
   But not for this alone.

I scarce know how, but thou dost tell
   Of sorrow—love, and bliss,
When, choked with tears, I breathed "farewell,"
   And sealed it with a kiss.

'T was winter—but the sunbeams shed
   Their light o'er sleeping earth;
Like smiles which stay, though life be fled—
   The type of happier birth!

The copse which closed the world was bare,
   Each flower and leaf had perished;
Save thou and we no life was there,
   No hope which once we cherished.

Who made the " we"—'t is, Bully, thou,
   And only thou canst say,
Thou only heard'st our parting vow,
   While throned upon thy spray.

Thou saw'st our tears in silence flow,
   Our love amidst despair,
Thou caught'st the essence of our woe,
   And murmured it in air.

For this, I 'll love thee till I die ,
   For this, my prayers are given
For love and life, with liberty,—
   Without, what 's earth or heaven ?

Sweet sylvan bird, till thou shalt die,
   I 'll wish thee, Bully, this;
And after death a purer sky,
   A tiny world of bliss.

———

Uni   *ft* ®

TO A LADY,

IN RETURN FOR SOME FLOWERS SHE HAD PAINTED.

———

I 've marked the print of fairy foot,
And wished the form had taken root,—
   A model cast in sand;—
But when had hopes the power to save?
My wishes found a watery grave
   As tides swept o'er the strand.—

I 've marked the flash of sparkling eye—
The tear half formed—the feeling sigh—
   Sweet echo of the mind,—
And wished for some magician's skill
To bid their beauties linger still,
   Like gems for ever shrined.—

On winter's eve, with raptured ear,
I've heard some strain to memory dear,
   Yet turned to weep the while;
To think that sounds, so loved—so sweet—
Were borne away on wings as fleet,
   As soft as Pleasure's smile.—

I 've gazed on flowers with fond delight,
And thought the chill of coming night
   Might doom them to decay;
And then I 've felt, that I would give
One year of life could they but live
   One other brilliant day.—

And, Lady, hast thou read my thought,
And has thy magic pencil wrought
   The hopes I dared not speak?
Thou hast!—thou hast!—before me lie
In fadeless tints, the form—the dye—
   The bloom from nature's cheek.

As bow the wretched to their shrine,
And clasp their beads with warmth divine,
   With fervour such as this
I bend before thy gifted wand,
I seize thy small and fairy hand,
   And breathe a poet's kiss.

Start not! blush not! for heaven is there,
And with it blends my spirit's prayer,
   Too pure to taint or die;
Its record calls a blessing down,
And asks for thee a rosy crown
   To mark thy destiny.

1828

Uni   *ft ®*

WELL-KNOWN LINES BY MACROBIUS.

———

" KISSING," says the New Monthly for 1821, " was an act of religion in ancient Rome. The nearest friend of a dying person performed the rite of securing his soul by a kiss, supposing that it escaped through his lips at the moment of expiration."

" Dulcemque florem spiritus (ejus puellæ)

Duco ex aperto tramite,

Anima tunc ægra et saucia

Concurrit ad labras mihi."

———

THROUGH lips—no more soft Love's retreat—

Her spirit flew to realms above,

Her fainting soul then rushed to meet

My last—sad—kiss of faithful love.

New Monthly, October, 1821

Uni   *ft* ®

Uni   *ft ®*

ON A TEAR.

Thou sparkling drop, as crystal clear,
  From whence thy source, and why thy birth?
Fall'st thou to hail the new-born year—
  O'erflows the cup of joy on earth?

Or hast thou been in sorrow nurst,
  Thy sire despair, which never spoke?
And hast thou now thy prison burst,
  To save a heart which else had broke?

One other year !—and memory swept
   O'er records of a life misspent;
Of time and talents lost, I wept,
   And heard a voice, which said, " Repent !"

I ne'er had thought to weep again,—
   Resigned to God's mysterious ways;
But holy thoughts came o'er the brain,
   And touched the spring of early days;

Such days as when the young, full heart
   In innocence and prayer o'erflows;
I felt a tear unbidden start,
   And thus my voice spontaneous rose :—

" On thee, O God ! my hopes are built,
   And when Thy voice shall call me hence,
May this pure drop outweigh my guilt,—
   It is the Tear of Penitence !"

Literary Gazette, Jan. 1, 1824.

ON THE

DEATH OF AN ORPHAN CHILD.

Uni   *ft ®*

ON THE

DEATH OF AN ORPHAN CHILD,

Who died of Consumption.

1816.

Sweet pledge of those once dear to me!
The blow is struck—and thou art free!
Thy little life of sufferings past
Is changed for one that's doomed to last,
To one, where joys unfading live,
Where blooms that peace the world can't give;
Where, if the pang thou here didst meet
Before the eye of memory fleet,
Such thoughts but rise in faintest gloom,
To gild with bliss thy happier doom:—
Then hush, my sighs; and cease, my tears!
'T were sin to weep thy shortened years,
For mercy dwells with God's decree;
The blow is struck—and thou art free!

Poor tender bud, it seemed as though
Thou wert not for this world of woe,
For scarce had she who gave thee birth
Received the crown of righteous worth,
Than sickness, like some worm accurst,
Attacked each blossom ere it burst,
And slowly—surely—preyed by stealth
Beneath thy rose of infant health :
Awhile indeed thou wert the ray
Which chased a father's grief away ;
The source of pleasure linked with care,
Of raptures which but parents share ;
But when that father's soul had fled,
More quickly drooped thy fainting head,
And thou didst learn to bless the blow
Which freed thee from this world of woe.

Yes—thou art fled, and thou art blest,
Each trial past—thy sufferings rest ;
Thou 'rt fled,—but O ! the poet's eye
Can pierce the realms of distant sky,
Can view—although he may not paint,
Such scenes as must in language faint,

For, ah! how faint were words to trace
Each change that marks a father's face,
When starts the tear, e'en from excess
Of overpowering happiness, —
And language ne'er could boast a charm
To tell how on that father's arm,
The wife—the mother—now reclines;
How soul with soul each link entwines;
How both now humbly bow the knee
In silent gaze of ecstasy,—
As pledges once on earth adored,
Are all again in heaven restored.

Though, Charlotte, still, methinks I see
The throes which sickness dealt to thee,
I feel, had fate delayed the blow,
Thou wouldst perchance have lived to know
Such keener pangs as rack the mind,
When those best loved prove most unkind:
And what are tears in childhood's day
But fleeting clouds o'er infant play?—
Like heat-drops from the summer sky,
This moment seen, the next gone by.

But oh! those bitter, scalding tears
Which burst from grief in later years,
Awhile resistless roll their tide,
And if at length their source be dried—
They cease—as falls the raging wind,
Which, ceasing, leaves a wreck behind:
And hadst thou run a longer course,
With feeling—passion—all in force,
Perchance—yet wherefore chances name,
Since life and sorrow are the same?
Then far be every selfish thought,
Which had been with *thy* misery bought,—
Oh! thine is now an happier sphere,
And prayers were sin that wished thee here.

CHARTLEY CASTLE,

AND

MARY QUEEN OF SCOTT'S GLASS.

Uni   *ft ®*

WH.M.___   etched by G.Ck.___

an Antique Glass ___

Supposed to have been in the possession of Mary Queen of Scotts

HB   the size of

CHARTLEY CASTLE,

AND

MARY QUEEN OF SCOTT'S GLASS.

———

THERE are some persons who possess a power of
fascination which acts like enchantment: we approach within their sphere, determinations are forgotten—reason is disarmed, and we only feel that
we have bowed to the magician's wand. Napoleon
possessed this power in an eminent degree; but in
the history of womankind, Mary Queen of Scotts
is recorded as the unrivalled enchantress. Her
final doom, which was decreed by our tyrannical
"Good Queen Bess;" her trials, while yet in the
glow of youth and beauty, have doubtless added
much to the sympathy which her fate has so generally awakened. They were as allies; but the force
by which she conquered consisted in that spell which

won all hearts,—a magic not to be described; but which was felt, and never could be forgotten by all who looked upon her features and listened to her voice. This was not a charm which passed like the dream of happiness,—once felt, it became a part of existence: the feeling was communicated, and they who listened warmed in the reflection, until succeeding ages with nearly one accord, regard with devotion the traces of her footsteps, and hold as sacred that which had ever been touched by the lovely martyr. Three fourths of the world would throw down the gauntlet as champions for her entire innocence; and few indeed amidst the remaining fourth, who do not feel a pleasure, at least a relief, in shutting their eyes against those " damning proofs" which the love of truth has brought to light. Chartley Castle was one of the many places where the ill-fated Mary sojourned as a prisoner: her stay there was short; but as elsewhere, the spot is consecrated to her memory, and in the wild and venerable park, a small mound is still pointed out as her favourite resort, where she would sit and listen for hours to the charms of music,—in remembrance of which, the said mound is to this day called " Fiddler's

Hill," a title, we confess, fatal to the ear of
romance, for though the finest masters of painting
have introduced angels as fiddling in heaven, there
is something in the word " fiddle "—in the form of
a " fiddle," most indisputably anti-romantic. But
what can a word avail against the enchantress—the
lovely and unfortunate? If there be one who doubt
the power of her spell, let him seek the spot, and
he will find that all association of the ridiculous is
absorbed in interest and compassion for the royal
prisoner. The spot itself seems to have been chosen
as commanding the most extensive view of the
surrounding country; and I can fancy her feelings
identified with some poor bird deprived of liberty,
forbidden to fly, yet deriving some happiness as
the sight ranged over the distant fields, and the ear
listened to the strains of other days, which floated
with the passing breeze, and met no prison walls
to check their flight. It was in the year 1821, that
I accompanied my friend —— on a visit to the
late Lord Tamworth, who was then staying at
Chartley Castle. Of the "real original" Castle
but little remains, and still less of the more recent
buildin.... .... Q.... .f S.... ... held in

captivity,—the former owed its strength to the hill
on which it stood, the latter to a deep and wide
moat by which it was entirely surrounded; but its
girdle of water, and the deeper source, which sup-
plied such powerful defence against the attack of
man, were unable to subdue the element of fire;
nearly the whole was burnt to the ground. A few
rooms had been restored from the ruins, to serve
as a sporting residence for our noble host, and, as
the cellars had escaped the conflagration, there
were the means of doing justice to the warmth of
his hospitable welcome, although, tradition says
that at the time of the fire, the ruling butler true
to his trust, and naturally thinking nothing so
valuable as good wine, selected the finest, and
braved the danger of the flames, in order to convey
his beloved charge to the custody of that piece of
water which we have already spoken of as supply-
ing the moat.   There is an old and somewhat
vulgar adage, as to the fish which escaped from the
fryingpan into the fire; and in this case the transi-
tion from fire to water proved equally fatal,—the
well filled bottles sank to such a depth of water
and mud, that they were lost beyond recovery. Day

Uni   ft ®

after day the disconsolate butler fished and fished,
without obtaining so much as a glorious nibble; the
extreme depth and the nature of the ground pre-
cluded the possibility of draining,—a measure, which
had it been possible, he would gladly have adopted
though at the risk of flooding the country around :
all was in vain, and there the rosy wine is still
blooming, unless, indeed, some river god has deemed
it fair plunder, and poured it forth at the banquet
of water nymphs and mud larks. Some months
previous to our arrival the surrounding moat had
been successfully drained, for the purpose of clear-
ing away the mud which had accumulated for ages;
in many parts it had attained to the depth of from
twenty to thirty feet, yielding to the farmer a rich
harvest, and the antiquarian a mine of endless
wealth; but alas ! no Dr. Dryasdust was near, to
watch over the sacrilegious shovels as they broke
upon the slumbering relics, and cast them aside
with reckless indifference: there were, it must be
allowed, some exceptions to this Gothic devastation,
and things, which the farmer knew to have no
positive power of vegetation, were collected and
preserv   and

shields in infinite variety; curious and elegantly-
formed drinking vessels; immense pewter dishes,
inlaid with gold, after the Chinese fashion of intro-
ducing mother-of-pearl upon the black-ground of
their brilliant varnish, and also some of the moun-
tain of empty bottles discovered opposite to the
door of the ancient butlery—there, tell-tale remains
of departed spirits seemed to have been collected
from every known part of the world: some were
perfect Patagonians; others, as the old song says,
" though very little fellows," were doubtless " of
right good stuff;" some with the neck of a crane,
others round and apoplectic as an overfed alderman; but their chief curiosity arose, not from the
shapes, which would have puzzled a mathematician,
but from a thin regular coating which had formed
in the course of years, and which, when dry, as-
sumed the splendour of the peacock's tail, and
exhibited the prismatic colours as we see them dis-
played in the oriental shells.—Yet what were these
but atoms in infinity? the mud, teeming with curi-
osities, had been carted away, spread upon acres
and acres of land, and afterwards carefully picked
over by labourers, who carried their collection to

fill up the deepest cart ruts. Neither I nor my friend positively fainted when we heard the fatal tale, we had enough of strength to inquire whether it were yet too late to sally forth and rescue,—" a something might be saved," was the cheering reply, and early the next morning we took the field. On our march, what desolation met the eye!— to Dr. Dryasdust, the Car of Juggernaut could scarcely have caused a greater pang than the track marked by the crushing waggon. We hurried on, and soon arrived at some fields where the remains of other days had not been gathered to such inglorious sepulchre; the sun and rain had whitened the skeletons, which in a large proportion bore witness to the determined attacks in the butlery:—on a sudden our attention was directed to the Glass represented in the annexed etching. Its figure and style bespoke the refinement of "auld lang syne." We read the first two lines:

> " Je songe tous jours a vous,
> Je suis tout a fait sensible,"—

and at the same moment our imaginations identified. . . . . Mary Queen

of Scots. It was the language of her beloved
France; it was the "gentilezza,"—the tone of her
feelings: we thought then, and have since ascer-
tained, that the very writing accorded with the
fac-similes which have been handed down to pos-
terity. Beneath these lines, were two others, con-
fessing the spell which won all hearts: the less
polished nature of some Englishman—it might
have been of her gaoler—was touched to softness,
blessed the lovely hand which had traced the passing thought, and found relief by expressing the
sympathy awakened.

> " Blessed be the hand which wrote it,
>   I with you may be thought it."

Let the sceptic doubt, and call for proofs: I wish
for no more. In those days but few could write;
the letters must have been cut by the pointed
diamond,—a pen worthy of a royal hand. At all
events, since I feel a happiness in believing I have
touched the glass which had been pressed by the
loveliest lips that ever spoke, let me enjoy my
faith, though it be delusion.

TO * * *

ON HER BIRTH-DAY.

Uni   *ft ®*

TO * * *

ON HER BIRTH-DAY.

———

The Blackbird's lay has died away;
A long—long night has checked his flight,
   And grief has chained his drooping wing;
And she whose praise, in happier days,
Called the varied note from his warbling throat,
   No longer bids the minstrel sing.

And the wintry blast o'er his hopes has past:
And his crest of pride, and the joyous tide
   Which glanced in the sparkling eye,
Ne'er more shall be seen in the woodland green;
Wit—feeling—thought, are as things of nought,
   For all has been, I have left to die.

But the fetter and yoke of the world shall be broke,
The hour must quickly be when the soul shall be
    free,
    And for worlds of sunny bliss her wings shall be
       spread;
And if thought turn away from the hope of this day,
'T is e'en amidst despair to offer up a prayer
    For her who awakes all the dreams which have
      fled.

And the Merle's last strain is for thee, dear Jane!
And his prayer is now, that thy virgin brow,
    And the eyes of soul with their dark lash veiled,
May for years be bright with their gay, pure light;
That the blessing of heaven to thy path be given;
    And for years, as now, may thy birth be hailed!

    Nov. 3, 1826.

TO ——,

ON HER BIRTH-DAY.

———

Twelve months ago, November third,
The spirit moved an idle bird,
   Whom Englishmen call " Black," *
To hail the day in blithest strain,
In honour of *la petite* Jane :
   But he had lost the knack.

———

* It is scarcely necessary to remind the reader, that
" Merle " is originally French, though sometimes used as
an English word. The " Merle " here alluded to, is most
decidedly French in origin, seeing that, after the revocation
of the Edict of Nantes, his grandfather was obliged to fly from
home — country—every native haunt, and seek refuge from
that bird of prey, Louis XIV., in this happier land. The
adopted motto of " Le Merle aime la liberté," proves that the
love of joke mingled with the love of liberty. The latter is
certainly inherited by the race of Blackbirds, and for the
reader's sake. I humbly hope that they are not quite wanting
in the fore

He sought the woods—the silent dell,
Where Inspiration used to dwell,
   But she was not at home;
He called on Fancy—sent his card;
They both denied themselves: 't was hard!
   Nor thought nor verse would come.

Where next to call?—He called to view
The days when Wit and all his crew
   Were his especial cronies;
When life was young, and galloped past
As merrily, and quite as fast,
   As Will and Regy's ponies.

The past arose; his feelings throbbed,
His very heart with pleasure sobbed,
   To see such visions float:
But soon, alas! too soon they sank,
Again he felt the world a blank,
   And sorrow filled his throat.

Thus sadly musing on his perch,
He spied, beneath a weeping birch,*
　　Miss Melancholy sitting;
And "Come," she cried, "take off your hat,
The while we have some sober chat,
　　And I pursue my knitting."

He heard the call, and, bold as Platoff,
He marched, but could not take his hat off,
　　Because—he had no hat on;
Forthwith the nymph of tears and sighs,
Wiped first her nose, and then her eyes,
　　And thus began to chat on.

" My sister Sorrow—by the way,
She 's sticking in your throat, you say,—
　　Well, she, and brother Pain,
And I—your most obedient,
Are each a sure ingredient
　　To work your good and gain.

* Ask any boy if the birch be not a more sorrowful tree
than the w il

" We come; the vicious halt on ruin's brink,
The heartless feel, the thoughtless think;
   We hint before we go,
That man was born to mourn—to die—
To hope a brighter, purer sky,
   And peace, unknown below.

" 'T is true, our visit oft offends,
Till mortals learn we are their friends;
   Like doctors with their phials,
We chasten those we love—of old,
You must have heard how man, like gold,
   Is purified by trials.

" Then leave awhile those idle flirts,
With laughing eyes, and tattered shirts,
   The Messrs. Wit and Mirth;
And here, amidst this pensive gloom,
Reflect upon that awful doom
   Ordained to all on earth."

She ceased; her talk inspired the bird
With thoughts as sad as though he 'd heard
   And felt the hangman's Jack close;
And darkly flowed the songster's lay,
Which was, we must confess, as gay
   And graceful as a black dose.

In haste he flew to Jane's Mamma,
Who complimented him with, " Psha!
   Your wits are on a shelf:
By one so happy, young, and good,
This song will not be understood,—
   I 'll keep it to myself."

A year has passed on rapid wing,
And still the Bird would gladly sing
   If he could tune his pipes;
He calls on Mirth to rule the day,
For Janey's sake to drive away
   All vinegar and swipes.

"All hail," he cries, "November ale!
If jugs are scarce, bring out a pail!—
   Hail frolic, bells, and plenty!
The Blackbird hails his Fairy Queen,
Whom Time pronounces just thirteen,—
   He wishes she were twenty.

"Beware!" he says, "for Winter's near,
Provision's scarce—the leaf is sear—
   And quickly fails the Christmas berry:
Then guard those lips of summer dye,
The Blackbird has a thievish eye,
   And doats on the red, red cherry!

"He has, 't is true, though comical,
Much wisdom anatomical,
   Knows how to steal each heart:*
Then shield a fruit he fondly spies,
Lest he should seize the virgin prize,
   To make his cherry tart.

---

* The black and white hearts of the garden, we presume.—
Query, should we read "steel?"

" And veil those eyes of kindling flash
Beneath their dark and silken lash,
  Like Cupid in his bower ;
Or there the bird will bask, and say,
Existence flows from their pure ray
  As light supports the flower.

" And hide those locks of glossy brown,
Or else within that tempting crown
  He 'll build his nest, and—guess—
As Yankies say—he 'd learnt to win
A crown of gems,—the very pin-
  Nacle of happiness !"

As thus he sang, with feelings high,
A whisper, soft as sorrow's sigh,
  Said, " Shame ! you naughty bird !
Are these the fruits of last year's schooling ?
'T is time that you should cease your fooling :
  Indeed, you 're half absurd !

" Your notes are bad !—your credit 's light !
Your bill 's dishonoured—bankrupt quite
   In sense as well as rhyme !
Your crest of pride is bald, or so,
What once was black is turned to snow,
   And this before your time !

" You should have been the Mother's voice,
And said, ' With trembling I rejoice;
   And while I hail the day,
I bow before the heavenly throne,
For blessings to my daughter shewn
   My adoration pay.

" ' But mothers know a mother's pride,
Her bosom's full and joyous tide,
   Which owns a source divine :
Yet may I ne'er, with fondness blind,
Forget to make the heart and mind
   As perfect as their shrine !

" ' And grant, O God, that health with joy,
That peace of mind, fair Virtue's boy,
    May guide her path for years!
Be thou to her the rainbow's smile,
The star which can all woes beguile,
    And light this vale of tears!' "

In cadence sweet, the whispered prayer
Was borne along the silent air—
    What more could Blackbird say then?
With humbled crest, and swelling throat,
He whistled forth a graver note—
    A fond and hearty—Amen!

Nov. 3, 1827.

Uni   ft ®

THE FIRST DAY OF SPRING.

———

Hail to the sun! the bright blue sky,
    For they are life to me,—
Triumphant Spring bids Winter fly,
    And Nature's soul is free.

Hail to the sun! whose heaven-born ray
    Hath roused each slumbering vein;
Life, love, and mirth with frolic sway
    Through all creation reign.

Through all—ay, all—for life and love
    Are felt by every flower;
For Venus and the turtle-dove
    The leaves have formed a bower.

Mark yonder buds, how side by side
    Their cheeks fond nestling to,
Who dare deny Love's magic tide
    Flows every fibre through?

And see those flowers of warmer hue,
    Like beauty fair and frail;
Whose coral lips young Phœbus woo
    And toy with every gale.

Behold you bee, whose roguish glance
    Has steered his fluttering wing;
He stops, and gives—O blessed chance!—
    A kiss without a sting.

Ah! what is spring with sun o'ercast?
    'T is youth with brow of age —
A summer's day with chilling blast?
    'T is Cupid turned a sage.

Then hail the sun, and summer's ray,
    Which bid soft feelings glow,
Which as they give one happy day,
    Wake sympathy for woe!

1824.

Uni   *ft ®*

PRAYER OF VENUS AND CUPID.

As Venus once within her arms
  Was fondling Master Cupid,
" The Bards," said she, "who sing our charms
  Are all too gross or stupid."

Her smiling Boy, cried " Banish care,
  Apollo we 'll implore :"
Could man or god refuse the prayer ?
  He heard—and gave them Moore !

Uni   *ft ®*

TO LAURA.

THANKS, *Laura*, thanks—the struggle's o'er,
   The fatal die is cast—
'T is sweet to know, we meet no more,
   That every hope is past!

The burst of fate may perhaps disarm
   The startled soul at first,
But soon, methinks, there flows a balm
   From words which speak the worst.

I feel within a calmness shed,
   The slumber of despair,
Each cord is snapt—the heart is dead

Alik

To be alone on earth—to feel
    There breathes not one below,
To weep my faults—to heaven appeal,
    Or turn one shaft of woe.

To mark, unmoved, the forked light,
    Whilst echoing thunders sound,
Yet feel a something near delight,
    As ruin stalks around.

To gaze on Nature's loveliest face,
    As smiles each living kind,
And then a mix'd emotion trace,
    Of hate with grief combined.

I, this had borne—ay, more than this
    Had not one sigh inspired;
For I have felt e'en nearest bliss
    Within myself retired.

But ah ! to view from eyes like thine,
    The glance that seemed all soul,
To list the sigh that from a shrine
    So pure, so softly stole ;

To view thee as some star of light,
  Some more than earthly spell,
With power to guide my soul aright,
  My varying passions quell;

To find such dreams as long had fled
  Once more resume their reign,
And feelings deemed for ever dead,
  Start forth to life again :

This could not last,—such thoughts were nurst
  Until the brain grew wild,
The trembling heart with feeling burst,
  The man became a child !

Yet need I blush that I could weep ?
  I scorn the Stoic's sneers—
If 't were a crime—my sin is deep,
  But few have shed such tears.

On hopes thus raised there weighed a stress
  Which made endurance vain—
They were not tempered by success,
  So soon were wrapt in twain

No power to wound the ear,
Fate's keenest stroke is weak 'gainst one
 With nought to hope, nor fear.

If e'er one wish—one prayer—I shape,
 'T is now by chance expressed;
I start when words like these escape,
 " O God! may *she* be blest!"

1816.

Uni   *ft* ®

⁣⁣* THE following "untoward event" occurred in a market-town in Warwickshire, some ten years since.

———

" WHO'LL buy two wild-ducks?" Bessy cried,—
A sceptic near, their race denied,—
  Bess, angry, turned her back :
That moment both the slandered birds,
To prove for once a woman's words,
  Flew off, and shouted " Quack !"

———

Note.—A similar circumstance occurred to a friend of mine last year, though attended with a happier result, thanks to copper caps and double barrel. Anxious to store his pond, he purchased some ducks, which, having arrived at their intended home, were set at liberty,—a word which they appeared to understand so thoroughly and prize so highly, that they immediately took flight, and chose a settlement of their own Luckily for my friend, it was at no great distance; and after a short pursuit, the wandering ducks paid the penalty of death, and were brought back to store the larder instead of the pond.

Uni   *ft ®*

LINES,

WRITTEN UPON REVISITING THE WYE AND TINTERN-ABBEY,
AFTER AN ABSENCE OF MANY YEARS.

———

WHEN life and hope were young, I dwelt
   In other worlds, I 'm sure:
Nae care I kenn'd,—and oh! I felt
   So happy—so secure!
Mine was indeed a world o' bliss,
I ween 't was little like to this;
Lang syne it was,—those days are flown—
It was a world indeed my own.

Dear, happy, artless hours of youth!
   When feeling ne'er was chill'd;
When kindness seem'd so like the truth,
   My very heart it thrill'd.
Oh! then I kenn'd a world of bliss,
But little, little like to this;
Lang syne it was,—those days are flown—
It was a world indeed my own.

To doubt, I had na' then been taught,
 Nor dreamt that man deceived;
And woman's lips, with sweetness fraught,
 Were lov'd—and aye believed.
Lang syne it was, and time has proved
This canna' be the world I loved;
I now but weep o'er pleasures flown,
O'er worlds which once were all my own.

Literary Gazette, 1823.

THE

WHITE PIGEON AND IRON CROW.

Uni   ft ®

Uni   *ft ®*

WHITE PIGEON AND IRON CROW,

"An o'er true Tale."

———

"THE mid-day of superstition is past; but while hope, fear, and sickness hold their empire on earth, the mind of man will occasionally be acted upon by a feeling, whose magic power has been broken, not destroyed—whose sun has set to rise no more, though some fainter rays may for ever continue to be reflected."—*An Ominous Legend*

——–

IT seems some twenty years or more,*
Since last I knocked at ———'s door—
   A friend esteemed of old,—
The servant said, " My master's out, sir,
" But, pray walk in, for I 've no doubt, sir,

—————— — - -- - — - -- - -   - --

* This is a poetical license,—in reality, not above six or seven ye

Uni   ft ®

Should Mistress e'er be told
That you were here, and would not halt,
She'll think it must have been my fault,
   And peradventure scold."

Well, well—thought I, I'll just peep in,
   But what was my surprise
To find mamma and daughter weeping
   As though they'd lose their eyes!
I asked—" what bless'd relation's dead?
Has some poor valued friend been wed?"

" Oh no!" they cried, "had that been all,
Well might our griefs be counted small,
   We shudder whilst we tell,—
Just now with dark, ill-omened clack,
Upon the rug, upon her back—
   A milk-white Pigeon fell!"

   Politeness bade me pause ;
At length I said, "it seems a folly,
To waste those tears, and melancholy
   For such a trifling cause,

No doubt this was,—I 'm perhaps absurd
   Because my notion's humbler—
A pigeon of a race I 've heard
   By breeders named, a tumbler !" ˟
Then added,—for I wished to soothe
The pangs which nought could quite remove,—
"Oh ! had this bird, which once was white,
Pursued some other, happier flight,

   Then ne'er had been her eye mauled:
She would have spared this trembling woe,
And feathers once as white as snow,
   Had ne'er been turned to pie-bald !"

" For shame !" they cried, "to treat with jest,
The signs of heaven—the tortured breast,
   This day will soon be rued :
Though you may smile, indeed it 's true,
Ne'er pigeon down a chimney flew,
   But something bad ensued."

It struck me then, the words were just,
Around was an infernal dust,
   I sneezed, and said with laughter,

" Such omens none can e'er dispute,
The rug—the carpet's spoiled with soot,
  Which, doubtless—followed after."

Some years had past, the winds were cold,
Or else my friend's great coat was old,
It matters not, or age, or season,
Or whatsoever was the reason—
And few indeed e'er name a true one—
Enough to know, he'd built a new one;
And such a one, since man was breeched,
The Fates ne'er cut, nor Graces stitched,
A lady vowed—of course, 't was truth—
Till then e'en from her earliest youth,
Papa ne'er looked so like Adonis,
Though he was much too wise to own this;
But what care thieves for Gods or Graces?
They 've small respect for things or places:
Scarce twice two weeks had passed away,
Since first that coat beheld the day,
When thieves attacked, per force and boring,
The house wherein my friend was snoring;
They fingered all that met their view,
Stole candlesticks and snuffers too,

Of minor spoons some dozen pairs—
The greater ones were all up stairs—
And Oh, remorseless villains! took
The great great-coat, which graced a hook !

Guess you, some maid absorbed in love—
    A waiting-maid, I mean—
Forgot to take these things above,
    Where they had safer been?
    I pr'ythee think not so—
These were with providence all wise,
To bless and glut the plunderers' eyes,
    On purpose left below ;
Lest finding all their labour lost,
Their project and their temper crost,
    With blasphemies emphatic,
They might have sworn to venture higher,
And mounted with intentions dire
    To ransack every attic.
When fame the doleful story brought,
I first shed tears, as friendship ought ;
Then said—my doubts shall now be ended,
My wavering faith be crushed or mended,
    So straightway sent to know,

Ere beams were cleft, ere bolts were burst,
Ere midnight rogues had done their worst,
If fate, on deeds like these intent,
For warning, down the chimney sent
   A monstrous Iron Crow!

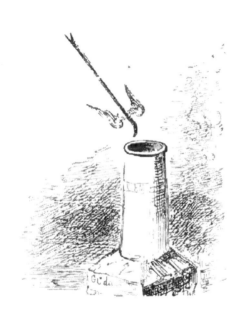

FAREWELL.

Uni   ft ®

Uni   *ft ®*

FAREWELL.

———

If some dread loss, some weight of heaviest woe,
Our every thought to one fixed centre bind;
Tho' moments then with lingering motion flow,
The hours unvaried leave no trace behind:
But ah! when some mark'd day recalls to mind
Such sparkling joys as once 't was wont to cast,
By contrast rous'd—with anguish more refin'd—
We scan those happier days which fled too fast,
And start—amazed to find that one more year is
     past.

One other year:—and how great change may be
Within that space!—how fears in endless train
With those few words arise! The past I see
In loveliest tints renewed; and then what pain
To think that she, whose smiles once formed the

To which my earthly hopes all seemed to cling,
Forgets the wretch who owned and blessed their
    reign,
Whilst one—yet hold—that thought might touch
    the string
To madness wound—and fear-struck Fancy droops
    her wing.

Enough—too much—to think those dreams are
    fled,
Which soothed my pangs when life seemed fleet-
    ing by,
For aye hadst thou, loved ——, cheered my bed,
E'en death methought had forced no yielding sigh:
And when, the one by every purest tie
Revered—the friend, than life itself more dear,
To some far happier world was borne on high,
Ah, then forlorn indeed! hadst thou been near,
Thy smiles methought had sometimes checked the
    falling tear.*

---

* The writer of the above had scarcely recovered from a
violent illness when he had a more severe trial in the loss of a
relation, who for years had been dear—as a father, friend, and
compan····

Uni   ft ®

But whence rose hopes like these which claim no
  base?

Does fate ordain that we must all pursue

A shade that lures, yet mocks, our idle chase?—

For though, perchance, when last I bade adieu,

One parting look spoke more than words could
  do—

And though, perchance, my hand were pressed
  again

With greater warmth than was to friendship
  due,

Yet these sweet thoughts revive their charms in
  vain.

As memory paints the frequent glance of cold dis-
  dain.

Said I—I dreamt?   And in a world like this

What's life itself but one continued dream,

From which how few, indeed, e'er wake to
  bliss?

What though awhile youth's livelier fancy
  teem

With views of endless joys! What though they

No fairy sketch in faithless tints arrayed!

Yet short's their reign as some bright meteor's
gleam,

For they—like flowers that deck the grave new-
made—*

But smile 'midst grief to-day, and with to-morrow
fade!

Then, perish thoughts which once were dear!—
despair

Must trace that word of saddest, wildest tone,

Which gains for thee—if ever yet the prayer

For others' weal were heard at Mercy's throne—

All bliss that may to one on earth be known:

Hadst thou, like me, e'er felt love's magic spell;

Had fate's stern will e'er bade thee part from one

Too dearly loved—Oh, then no need to tell!—

That fatal word—that prayer of agony's—Farewell!

1816.

TO MY WIFE,

ON HER BIRTH-DAY.

,

The pearl, though pure as virtue's tear,
The sparkling gems as crystal clear,
The chain-like webs of fairy gold,
Obey the rich—are bought and sold.
No—nought in air—from sea, from earth—
Shall hail the day which saw the birth
　　　　Of thee, my own, my Mary!

When poets feel the words they say,
Their fervent, pure, though simple lay
Outweighs the gems on regal brow;
And such the gift I offer now,—
" The warmest wish that heart can give,
The prayer to Heaven that thou mayst live
　　　　Happy and blest, my Mary!"

Uni   *ft ®*

LACONIC DESCRIPTION OF THE FIRE-WORSHIPPER IN MOORE'S "LALLA ROOKH."

Pro ré pauca loquar.—VIR.

THE sweet-heart of Hinda
Was burnt to a cinder;
And she, luckless daughter!—
Jumped into the water.

Uni   *ft ®*

TO LAURA.

Uni   *ft* ®

TO LAURA.

LINES WRITTEN AFTER A TRIFLING QUARREL.

———

No, Laura, no!—it is in vain!
 Those smiles cannot deceive me;
Thy thoughts will strike a chord of pain
 When I'm about to leave thee!

Thy looks—thy manner—all are changed:
 Yet grief will soon await thee.
Thy heart awhile may be estranged,

No, Laura, no!—too long—too well
    Thy every thought I've known;
I feel thy memory oft must dwell
    On scenes for ever flown.

Believe me—'t is no easy task,
    The truth thou canst not shroud
Beneath the shade of pleasure's mask,
    By mixing with the crowd.

E'en then I've seen a tear arise,
    And swell the vacant eye—
As feelings taken by surprise
    Forgot that mirth was nigh.

Ay, too, sometimes when most you mean
    To prove yourself offended,
A word of kindness drops between,
    Unguarded—unintended.

Go, seek for friends!—you'll soon find some
    Who charm by being new;
But years must pass and sorrows come
    Ere you can prove them true.

I've marked through sun and wintry wind
   With tenderness unceasing,
A woodbine round a sapling twined,
   Their love with years increasing;

I've marked—perchance with foolish pain—
   The woodman's fatal blow,
And seen those links of love remain,
   Though death had laid them low!

Thus, Laura, grew our early love—
   Unchanged through grief and joy,
Till time, methought, a link had wove,
   Which nought could e'er destroy:

And why should words, in anger spoken,
   Crush friendship formed by years?
Must hopes of future sun be broken—
   Because one cloud appears?

Each hour—as fate unweaves our lot—
   Some hope, some pleasure rifles:
And friends once gained—like heaven—should not
   Be thro

'T were harsh shouldst thou that bark condemn,
    Which rights when all seems lost;
Then pardon words I could not stem,
    Awhile in passion tost.

As seas close o'er the vessel's course,
    Thus souls like ours should blend;
Thus words which wound should lose their force,
    And angry feelings end.

Uni   *ft* ®

LINES

ADDRESSED TO A GENEVA WATCH.

Uni   *ft ®*

LINES

ADDRESSED TO A GENEVA WATCH,

PRESENTED TO MY MOTHER.

———

LITTLE bauble, adieu! gayest offspring of art,—
  I destine you now for another;
Go—and true to your trust, with all frankness
    impart
  The love which I feel—for a mother.

Though we part, it is not that despairing I seek
  To obtain from some fair one a vow,
Which the sweet lips of woman so firmly can
    speak,
  And th...

For no heavenly smile by your aid do I plead,
    Which I know but too well would not last,
Since a trifle could soon cause a frown to succeed,
    And my heaven be quickly o'ercast.

Purer far is the charge which to you I ascribe,
    And sacred's the homage I pay;
For the love of a mother demands not a bribe—
    Her smiles beam unclouded each day !

On yourself and the giver, then, credit reflect,
    And beware, lest your hands should deceive,
To which end, all your works must be far more
        correct
    Than are his whose advice you receive.

With the lot which awaits you contented remain,
    Or in value you're certain to fall,
For believe me—though strange it may seem—if
        you gain,
    You will soon be worth nothing at all.—

You must also remember, as part of your creed,
   That " not to obey is a crime,"
And when wanted to go, you must always proceed,
   And that too—without loss of time.

As an index of truth, when she looks on your face,
   And is taught how her time steals away,
Oh ! then whisper this truth—" even time has no
     space
   Which shall e'er know my love to decay."

   1811.

Uni   *ft ®*

SPEECH, &c.

.

Uni   *ft ®*

SPEECH

DELIVERED FROM THE THRONE OF HIS GRACIOUS MAJESTY
THE KING OF PETTY-FRANCE AND PICKPOCKETS.

.   .

WE look with pleasure to the confidence and
co-operation existing between ourselves and our
beloved subjects, and trust to their continuance,
from having been so often linked together by the
strongest ties.

As man is that superior animal which claims the
exclusive privilege of scratching himself all over,
we despise those idle alarmists who infer, because
our state is ticklish, that we must go to Old
Scratch.

Our arts are flourishing: but we have noticed
with alarm the elevation to which some of our

Uni   ft ®

worthy subjects have attained,—a height which must prove fatal to their lives and well-being, and which, we are willing to believe, was not originally contemplated by their wildest ambition.—We trust to see no more of this.

We look with complacency to our customs, and can assure the nation that our resources arising thence are rapidly increasing.

We recommend our council to persevere in the system of free trade, the blessing and profits of which stare us in the face: and the justice of making free with our neighbour's property is too palpable to require argument.

Our Continental alliances continue unshaken: with the United States we are as thick as two pick-pockets, and our colony of New South Wales bids fair to rival its Mother Country in clever researches; as botanists, they are collectively superior to our London College.

counts are most satisfactory.   Our prisons are well
regulated and respectably filled.   We there see to
advantage the march of intellect· the guilty are
taught to tread the steps which lead to health and
strength.   From our throne, we return thanks to
our well-beloved Mrs. Fry, trusting that our rising
generation will be innocent as the fry unborn, and
as ably protected from the snares of the Devil as
white-bait from the nets of man, thanks to our
merciful Court of Aldermen.

We beg to calm the public mind, by assuring
our well-beloved subjects, that a Popish plot does
not exist : we confess to the curious fact of finding
near our throne a bag-full of skeletons, a dark
lantern, and Berry's phosphorus box.   We ordered
the former to be buried in silence, or preserved as
a memento of our calling; the two latter we have
retained for the benefit of our ministry.

To our Lords and Commons we look forward
with confidence for the continuance of such liberal
supplies as the exigences of our state require,
trusting that our taxes will be levied with such

Uni   ft ®

delicacy and tenderness, that the money of the rich will pass from their pockets, and the loss be unfelt.

We conclude by stating the only pleasant conviction we ever arrived at,—namely, that *We*, in the purity of *our* conscience, consider Reform to be utterly unnecessary.

———

Note.—This is the age of cant, and endless are the perversions effected under that mask.—" Prevention is better than cure;" I therefore think it wise to say, that the above was written two years since; and although it may be deemed a merry satire on the style of composition which usually pervades the Speech put into the King's mouth, I should be the last man to insult, directly or indirectly, one who is so justly beloved and respected as our present monarch, King William the Fourth.

LINES, &c.

LINES

WRITTEN BY GUIDO, DURING EXILE AND SICKNESS.

———

Perch' io non spero di tornar giammai,
  Ballatetta, in Toscana,
  Va tu leggiera, e piana
  Dritta alla donna mia.
    *   *   *

Tu voce sbigottita, e deboletta,
Ch' esci piangendo dello cor dolente,
Con l'anima' e con questa ballatetta
Va ragionando della strutta mente.
Voi troverete una donna piacente
Di sì dolce intelletto
Che vi sarà diletto
Starle davanti ognora.
Anima e tu l'adora
Sempre nel suo valore.—
         *   *

TRANSLATION.

Since I've no hope, my little lay,
  To see my country more,
Go, softly haste, and ever stay
  With her whom I adore.—

          *   *   *   *

And thou, my voice,—desponding, weak,
That canst but tones of sorrow speak,
With this my lay and soul take flight,
Go tell, the mind is sunk in night·
And thou shalt then a lady meet
Of intellect so passing sweet,
      That to be near
      Shall heaven appear:
My soul and thou bow down before her,
  And for her worth for aye adore her!

Tu senti, ballatetta, che la morte
Mi stringe sì, che vita m'abbandona;
E senti come 'l cor si sbatte forte
Per quel, che ciascun spirito ragiona;
Tant' è distrutta già la mia persona,
Ch' i' non posso soffrire:
Se tu mi vuoi servire
Mena l'anima teco,
Molto di ciò ti prego,
Quando uscirà del core.—

Thou feelest now, my little lay,
That death hath struck—life ebbs away;
Thou feel'st how strongly beats my heart
    With every breath that speaketh now:
So deeply grief hath played her part,
    She can inflict no further blow.
If thou hast still the wish to serve,
    Lead forth my soul with thee;
O this my fervent prayer observe,
    When from my heart 't is free!

1822.

Uni   *ft ®*

A GREEK EPIGRAM.

THE mother has forgot her first-born pledge
    To dream of one beneath a distant sky :
When, lo ! the child has gained the cliff's loose
    edge !
    Oh, stir not !—speak not !—or the boy must die.
With all a mother's lore, she bared her panting
    breast,
The infant saw it, sought it, and was saved and
    blest !

Literary Gazette, August, 1822

Uni   ft ®

CONSOLATION FOR THE LOSS OF A NEW HAT.

———

Poor Bird has lost his dandy hat,—
His friends all weep a loss like that,
    And shew their love and wit,
By saying—" We had felt less shock,
If he had merely lost the block
    His hat was wont to fit."

Uni   ft ®

IN REMEMBRANCE OF

MY DOG GELERT.

IN REMEMBRANCE OF MY DOG GELERT.

HUMBLE's the mark—the hand can boast no skill,
Which now would fain this last sad office fill,
Would strive, my much-loved dog, thy worth to
    save,
And bid thy memory live beyond the grave!

Should chance, kind stranger, lead thy footstep
    nigh,
Blush not to grant one tributary sigh;
Trust me, a tear might be with justice paid,
For here my brave, my faithful GELERT's laid!

LINES

WRITTEN UNDERNEATH THE FOREGOING,

SEEING THEM BADLY PRINTED ON A SMALL PIECE OF WOOD

You say, " the hand can boast no skill!"
Who sees the printing, dearest Will,
   That truth might quickly guess:
But wherefore stick the lines up here?——
Unless to make it also clear
   The head can boast still less!

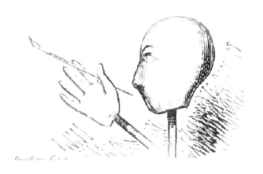

Uni   *ft ®*

HASTY PICTURE

or

A CITY AND ITS INHABITANTS.

Uni   *ft ®*

HASTY PICTURE OF A CITY AND ITS INHABITANTS.

———

Some new houses of red brick—of mud, wood, and
plaster :

Many old ones, which threaten some grievous dis-
aster ;

Many streets without pavement—one or two with
sad rough ones ;

With a few pretty young girls, and with many old
tough ones :

Many streets which allow just one cart to go
through ;

Just one street big enough, by good luck, to hold
two—

Uni   ft ®

By good luck, for in fear so much ground should
   be waste,
Here the market they hold — here display their
   good taste,
And with baskets, old women, stalls, cabbage and
   meat,
For six months they block up the one side of the
   street—
Then they change, lest one side should dare laugh
   at the other,
And the rest of the year deal as wisely with
   t'other.*

Nor is this the sole rule which a stranger sur-
   prises,
Where the time for rejoicing 's the week of assizes,
Where the ladies all feelings of woman forego,
Fancy music in chains—find a pleasure in woe !

---

* It is the custom in this city to hold the market in the
only tolerable street for six months on the one side, and the
other six on the other side.

And resort to the court to be seen, and to stare,
And to laugh while resounds the wild shriek of
　　despair;*
Where, by customs ordained, look a girl in the face,
And forthwith yours is voted a desperate case—
Merely offer an arm, all who near you may stand,
By the morrow will swear that you offered your hand!
Where, at balls so much rudeness and riot's dis-
　　played,
Such disputes from all sides for precedency made,
That you're standing three deep—when you stand
　　in your place,
When your turn comes to dance, dancing's out of
　　the case;

---

* In most county towns, it is the custom for ladies to frequent the courts of justice as a morning's lounge. At Exeter
it seems to be the principal amusement; and with little regard
to feeling or delicacy, the criminal hall is preferred.—This
was written in 1818, and it would appear that the same
custom is preserved. It was only at the last assizes that a
prisoner cut his throat in the dock, while the jury were delibe-
rating on their verdict. and, say the papers, "the court was
principally filled by ladies."

Where, such learning and skill are so wondrously
   shewn,
That e'en all understand all affairs—but their own!
Hold, enough!—other features there surely need
   not,—
Should one reader still doubt of the name of this
   spot,
Where there's little to please one, and not much
   to vex one,—
'T is the pride of the West—'t is—in short, it is—
   Exon!

WRITTEN IN PENCIL,

ON RECEIVING A "SOUVENIR" FROM A LADY WHO HAD OFTEN
REQUESTED SOME LINES FOR HER ALBUM.

———

THE fair skin of an ass, and a pencil of lead!
Why, the hint is enough to raise words from the
    dead,—
      Your satire could not fail!
Like a woman, at last you have carried your end,—
So my thanks, dearest ——, in six verses I send,
      As heavy as they 're frail!

Uni   ft ®

Uni *ft ®*

Uni   *ft ®*

THE ARAB GRAY.

———

Quick! quick! my steed, thy aid I need,
    There is fire beneath my brow!
Like the gasp of death, is my heaving breath,
    Let me vault to my saddle bow.

Away! away! my Arab gray,
    For life is in thy spring,
The rushing wind, we'll leave behind,
    And mock the eagle's wing.

By the roaring main, o'er the sandy plain,
    Now we cleave the air!
And it seems in our flight, like the dew of the night
    To my

O'er the hills we sweep ! in thy bounding leap
 There's a rush of joyous tide—
Now I live once more, as I've done before,
 In the strength of lonely pride.

Am I then alone ?—a monarch on the throne,
 In loneliness may move;
I feel my Arab's bound, I see my faithful hound,
 I've two on earth to love !

Thanks ! thanks! my gray, our course we'll stay,
 Thou shalt drink at the shady well;
Thy nostrils are spread, thy veins are ruby red,
 We will rest in the lonely dell.

Blessed spirit of good, thy dwelling's in the wood,
 Thy path by the world untrod;
Now my passions thou hast quelled, and the heart
  which rebelled,
 Has turned all its thoughts to God.

Dec 28, 1828.

ON THE FAILURE OF TWO SUCCESSIVE HAY HARVESTS.

———

Though we, last year, had sun enough, alas!
But little hay was made—for want of grass:
This year's as bad; for now—the devil take it!
We've grass enough, yet want—a sun to make it.

TO A LADY

WHO REQUESTED SOME LINES IN RETURN FOR A HEAD
BEAUTIFULLY DRAWN.

———

" SWEET Mary of the jet-black steed,"
When thou canst condescend to plead,
   Refusal must be vain !—
And if I fail, the fault's with thee,
My head is all a head should be,
   Save—that it wants a brain.

Uni   ft ®

Uni   *ft ®*

MY NATAL DAY.

Heavily broke the hour of dawn
Which told another year was gone !
And the sun was hid
By the thunder's lid ;
No light was there
But the forked glare,
As the dark dense clouds
Burst their sable shrouds ;
And the earthquake arose
Like a giant from repose,
And shivered at its birth
The bands of the earth ;
And the granite rocks like an aspen shook,
And rivers were shrunk to a babbling brook,
Then the sea upreared with its foaming head,
And cities were sunk in the ocean's bed.

And I felt my heart accord
With the spirits then abroad;
My pulse was wild as the reckless wind,
And passions swept o'er my reeling mind,
My thoughts were dark as the thunder's scowl,
And the withering blast with its deep, deep howl;
The shriek and the yell of agonized fear
Like harmony fell on my feverish ear;
For hatred—love—revenge—despair,
And madness springing from its startled lair,
Ay, these it was, o'er heart and brain,
Like tyrants held their troubled reign—
                And this was my natal day!

'T was eve—a voice from Heaven was sent,
Which stilled each warring element,
And bade them cease;
And all was peace.*—
The hum of the bee was heard from afar,
And, fixed in his flight, like a diamond star,

The pigmy bird—the gentle breeze
Which kissed the tears from the drooping trees,
And all beneath the smiling sky
With one accord made melody.—
Then the parting sun his radiance shed,
On the couch where the wind had pillowed his head,
And nature was hushed in the slumber of night,
And Time passing on, thus marked in his flight
        The close of my natal day!

Like the shadow of death, night around me fell,
And my brow was calmed by the midnight's spell,
And I hallowed the sleep of the dreaming air,
And in silence breathed a sinner's prayer,
For my spirit was bowed to the will of God.
As the rock which awoke to the Prophet's rod,
My heart was touched, and gushing tears
Renewed the spring concealed for years;
They fell as the dew to the fevered ground,
My agony passed—yet I looked around,
And I envied the flowers, whose griefs are as light
As the shadow that's cast by the eagle's flight,
For never more can my tears be dry,

Whose voice could charm as the gentle breeze
Ah! never more can I hope for these!
My sun is set in the winter of woe,
The dreams of youth with their sunny glow
Can rise no more,—my lonely bark
Flags on through hours, cold, dreary, dark,
        And journeys to the grave!

September 18, 1827.

FINAL.

TO THE READER.

In sportive mood our page began,
From light to grave the change has ran,
   And now we reach the end:
If I have touched a mournful theme,
The " finis " of an earthly dream,
   Forgive,—and call me friend.

As sorrow waits on all below,
If I have chased a moment's woe,
   I have not lost my end;
And, Reader, thou may'st bless the day
Bestowed upon an idle lay,
   And call the minstrel, friend.

The blackbird is no rara avis—
No dying strain to " Merle or Mavis,"
   Does fate in pity lend;
Or sweet should be his parting note,
The words which tremble in his throat,

& Manning & Co., Printers, London-House Yard, St. Paul's

Uni   *ft ®*

Uni   *ft ®*

Uni   *ft* ®